MAKERS

Retold by Tony Bradman
Series Advisor Professor Kimberley Reynolds
Illustrated by Steve Horrocks

OXFORD
UNIVERSITY PRESS

Letter from the Author

I love reading stories, and I love writing them too. My favourite stories are those about clever characters who 'live on their wits'.

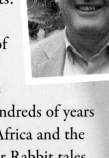

The stories in this book are originally from different parts of the world, but they're also old. The stories about Till Owlglass were being told in Germany hundreds of years ago. Anansi comes from West Africa and the Caribbean islands. And the Brer Rabbit tales are from the United States.

Each of the characters is what we call a 'trickster' – they like to cause as much mischief as possible. But they usually play tricks on characters who aren't very nice, so we feel they get what they deserve. You'll wonder – will the trickster character succeed? Then you'll be surprised by their cleverness. And you'll laugh to see the villains defeated. Stories don't really get any better than that, do they?

Tony Bradman

Till Owlglass and
the Painting

There was once a boy called Till Owlglass who was full of mischief. He lived in Germany a long time ago and people have been talking about his tricks ever since.

Till travelled from town to town looking for fun, and one fine day, he arrived in a place called Marburg. A rich lord – the new Count of Hesse – lived in a large palace there with his wife and lots of servants. Till decided to pay this Count a visit.

At first, the palace guards didn't want to let him in, but that was no problem for Till. His golden tongue soon convinced the guards that he was a Very Important Person, and they opened the gate.

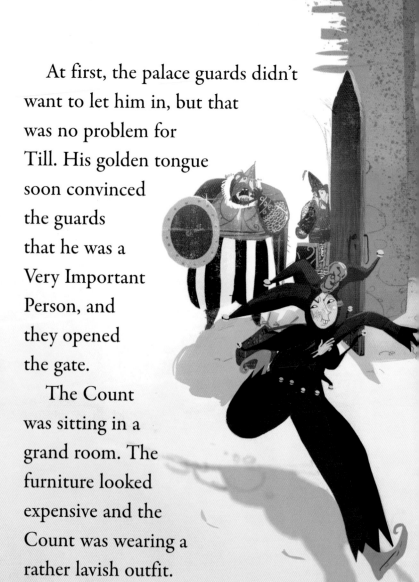

The Count was sitting in a grand room. The furniture looked expensive and the Count was wearing a rather lavish outfit.

'Welcome to my palace,' said the Count. 'My servants tell me you're a Very Important Person, but they didn't say exactly what you do. Of course, I'm a Very Important Person, too. Why, I'm descended from a long line of Very Important People ... '

Till listened while the Count droned on and on about his family and how 'noble' his ancestors were. Now Till didn't like snobs, and he always knew when someone was fibbing – after all, he was pretty good at it himself. He had a feeling the Count had made up the whole story so his family would sound more impressive.

'Actually, I paint pictures,' said Till when the Count stopped to draw breath.

'Is that so?' said the Count, suddenly interested. 'What kind of pictures?'

'Oh, pictures of noble families,' said Till. 'I could paint yours if you like.'

'That would be excellent!' said the Count, beaming. 'Hang on, how do I know you're any good?' he scowled. 'Do you have some pictures you can show me?'

'Actually, I do,' said Till. It just so happened that he did have a few with him – although he hadn't painted them himself. He'd picked them up on a trip to Flanders. You never knew what might come in handy when you were a trickster.

'These pictures are wonderful!' said the Count. 'But I would like something much bigger – a painting that covers one entire wall of my Great Hall so everyone can see how noble my family is! Could you do that? And how much would you charge?'

'Oh, you get my special discount for really noble customers,' said Till. 'It will cost you four hundred gold marks, half upfront. But there's one condition. You have to leave me alone – no one is allowed to see the picture until it's finished, not even you.'

'Why, what sensitive creatures you artists are!' said the Count. 'Of course, we will do whatever you say.'

Till just smiled. He sent a couple of the Count's servants out to buy all the things an artist would need – paints and brushes, and some ladders because it was going to be a *big* picture. Then he went into the Great Hall and locked the doors.

The Count was very excited and so was his wife, the Countess, when he told her. She was as much of a snob as her husband.

Till came out later for lunch, and later still for dinner, but he kept the doors locked and slept in the Great Hall at night. He did the same the next day, and the day after, and pretty soon, a week had gone by.

'How much longer will it take?' said the Countess. 'I'm dying to see it.'

'Me too,' said the Count. 'But I don't think you can hurry these artists ... '

Another week went by, then another, and another. By now, the Count and Countess were almost mad with impatience and so was everyone else in the palace.

At last, the Count simply couldn't stand it any more, and one lunchtime he lay in wait for Till.

'I know I'm not supposed to see it yet,' he said. 'But can I just have a peek?'

Till sighed. 'Oh, very well,' he said. 'It's nearly finished anyway.'

They went into the Great Hall. The wall with the picture was covered by a large curtain. Till took one corner and was about to pull it aside, but then he paused.

'I hope you don't mind, but I've been adding a special secret ingredient to the paint,' he said. 'Only those people descended from a truly noble family – like yours, of course – will be able to see the picture. To everybody else, it will be invisible.'

'Er ... really?' squeaked the Count. 'That's very nice of you, but that's not—'

He didn't have time to say anything else before Till swept back the curtain. 'Here's the Roman Emperor you told me you were descended from,' said Till, pointing at the wall. 'Here's that king, and the queen you mentioned. So – what do you think?'

The Count opened his mouth, but no words came out. To his utter horror, all he could see was ... a perfectly blank wall! But he couldn't say that, could he?

18

'Er … I … I think … '
he spluttered. 'It's
absolutely brilliant!' he
said at last. 'You've
managed to capture my
family perfectly. Well,
I'll, er … leave you to
it then … '

He scuttled away and as soon as he had gone, Till burst out laughing. Of course, there was no picture on the wall – Till hadn't painted a single thing. In fact, he had spent the last four weeks reading and relaxing between his lovely free meals.

As soon as the Countess
heard the Count had been in
the Great Hall, she demanded
to see the picture as well. Till
gave her the same warning
and the same thing happened.
When Till pulled back the
curtain, she saw ... a blank
wall. She was horrified like
her husband, but quickly said
the painting was wonderful.

That was the beauty of Till's trick. Because the Count and Countess were both such snobs, neither could admit the truth. But someone else in the palace wasn't so easily fooled. One of the servants was a jester, a woman whose job it was to make the Count and Countess laugh. She went to the Great Hall to look at the 'picture' herself.

'No, I can't see it,' she said. 'But my family isn't noble, so I wasn't expecting to. Mind you, that wall is *so* blank I can hardly believe there's a picture on it at all.'

She turned to Till and gave him a hard look – but his face gave nothing away.

That afternoon, Till told the Count that the picture was finished and asked for the rest of his money. A little later, he heard raised voices coming from the Great Hall. It seemed the jester had told the Countess she thought that Till's 'picture' was nothing but a trick.

'You idiot!' the Countess yelled at the Count. 'He's made a fool of you!'

'What about you?' the Count yelled back. 'You said your family was noble!'

Of course the Count sent his men to arrest the trickster ...

But as always, Till was long gone, jingling the coins in his pocket.

Anansi and the Antelope Baby

Everybody has heard about Anansi the Spider and his tricks, of course. He's the eight-legged King of Mischief and he's never short of ideas for having fun, usually at the expense of other creatures. But even he needs some help from time to time – and that's when you might get to see he has a decent side to his character as well.

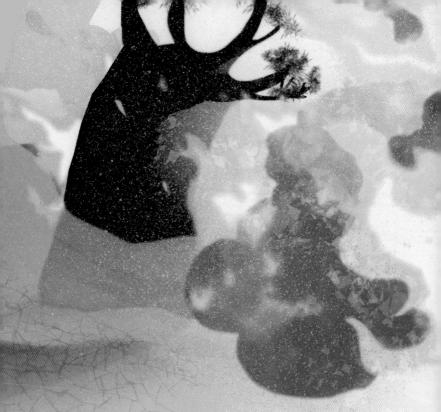

One day, he was hanging around in a bush, spinning a web, as spiders do. Anansi was thinking about all the tricks he might play when suddenly he smelled smoke. He scrambled to the top of the bush to find out what was going on and his eyes nearly popped out. The forest was on fire and a wall of flame was heading his way!

'Oh no, I'm in big trouble now!' Anansi muttered to himself. 'My little legs will never outrun that fire. What can I do?'

All the animals in the forest were running away. Anansi called out to each one as they rushed past – 'Help me, please!' – but none of them did as he asked. Anansi didn't have many friends because

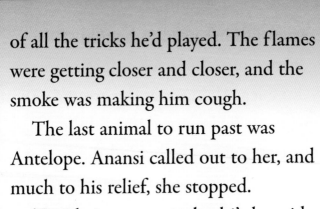

of all the tricks he'd played. The flames were getting closer and closer, and the smoke was making him cough.

The last animal to run past was Antelope. Anansi called out to her, and much to his relief, she stopped.

'Quick, jump on my back!' she said. 'We don't have much time!'

Anansi didn't need to be told twice.
He leaped onto her back and she ran off,
her long legs flying over the ground. Anansi
clung on as he bounced up and down.
The flames were just behind them, and
he thought they weren't going to make it,
but they did. They reached the edge of
the forest where the fire stopped.

'Phew, that
was close!' said
Anansi, lowering
himself to the
ground. 'I can't
thank you enough,
Antelope. If you ever
need any help, you can
certainly count on me.'

'That's very kind of you,
Anansi,' said Antelope. 'Take
care of yourself – cheerio!'

Anansi watched her go, then went on his way himself. Time passed and things settled down again. The forest started growing, all the animals came back, and Anansi got up to his usual mischief. But he had a soft spot for Antelope and never tried any tricks on her or her new baby – a beautiful little creature she clearly adored.

One day, Anansi was hanging around in a tree when he saw the two of them.

'You stay here, Baby,' Anansi heard Antelope say as she tucked him under a bush. 'I'm going to get some of that sweet grass you love. Don't worry, I won't be long.'

Then she bounded off. Anansi turned
to leave, but then he saw two hunters come
out from behind a nearby rock! Anansi hid
behind the tree so they wouldn't spot him.

'Come on, after her!' said the first hunter.
'We can return for the baby later.'

Anansi watched them go and felt worried about his friend. He decided she would probably be all right, though – she could run like the wind and she had escaped hunters before. But what if she kept going, thinking she was leading them away from Baby? The hunters would just give up the chase and come back for him.

Anansi realized that only *he* could save Baby – but what could he do? Anansi desperately racked his brains ... and at last,

it came to him. What if he spun a web around the bush so the hunters couldn't see Baby?

Anansi quickly got to work, but the hunters came back before he'd finished. Anansi stopped what he was doing and watched them nervously from behind a leaf. They looked rather cross, so Anansi guessed Antelope had escaped.

'Where's the baby?' said the first hunter. 'This was the place, wasn't it?' 'Yes, I thought he was under this bush,' said the second hunter. 'Although it looks different now – it didn't have this spider web on it.'

'You're right,' said the first hunter. 'But let's have a closer look ... '

Anansi felt a surge of panic – he had to finish the web! He started spinning as fast as he could, keeping one step ahead of them as they walked round the bush.

It was touch and go ... but he got the whole bush covered just in time. Then he lowered himself to the ground beside Baby and waited, holding his breath.

'No, this can't be the same bush,' said the first hunter at last.

'Come on then,' said the second hunter. 'Let's look elsewhere.'

Anansi only breathed out
once he knew the hunters had gone.
At that moment, Antelope came
running up. 'Baby!' she cried out.
'Where are you, Baby?'

'Don't worry, Antelope,' said Anansi,
tugging a hole in the web. 'Here he is!'

Anansi told Antelope what had
happened and she was very relieved.

'Oh, Anansi,' she said. 'I'll never be
able to thank you enough!'

'Think nothing of it,' said Anansi.
'That's what friends are for.'

The other animals didn't believe it
when Antelope told them he'd said that ...

But for once, the King of Mischief
really, really
meant it!

Brer Rabbit and the Well

It was a beautiful day and the sun was shining down on Brer Rabbit as he hopped through the fields. Now usually he would be looking for someone to play a trick on. But he felt very hot, so he was looking for something cool to drink instead.

At last, he came to an old well. You had to lower the bucket and fill it with water, then haul it back up again to drink. Brer Rabbit started to do that ... but then he stopped.

How lovely it would be to get right into the water, he thought.

So he jumped on a bucket and **whizzed** down. Another bucket passed him on the way, shooting upwards, but he took no notice. He hit the water with a great **splash**, and swam and drank, and drank and swam until he felt much cooler.

Then a nasty thought occurred to him. He realized he couldn't haul himself out of the well – and his bucket wouldn't go up until someone lowered the other one.

'Oh, no!'
he said. 'I could
be trapped down
here for days.
Help! Help!'

'You must be
joking, Brer Rabbit,'
said a mocking voice
far above him.

Brer Rabbit looked up and saw
that it was Brer Fox.

'I've been watching you,' Brer Fox
continued, 'and I know you can't get out.
But you can stay there forever as far as
I'm concerned!'

Things were going from bad to worse for Brer Rabbit. He'd played a lot of tricks on Brer Fox, so he knew he'd get no help from him. But then Brer Rabbit had an idea. Brer Fox was very greedy – he simply couldn't resist the offer of food.

'Oh well,' he said. 'I suppose I'll just have to eat all these fish myself.'

'Fish?' said Brer Fox. 'Er ... what are they like? Are they very tasty?'

'You'd better come down and find out for yourself,' said Brer Rabbit. 'All you have to do is jump in that bucket and you'll soon be having a fishy feast!'

'Fantastic!' said Brer Fox. He jumped on the bucket at the top of the well and **whizzed** down. Brer Rabbit had already made sure he was sitting on the other bucket, so he **whizzed** up. The two of them passed each other halfway.

Brer Fox hit the water with a big **splash** and jumped off the bucket.

'Hey, hang on a minute,' he yelled. 'I don't see any fish down here ... '

'Ah, I might have been fibbing about that,' said Brer Rabbit. 'Bye!'

Then he hopped away with a huge smile on his face.